SMART SCIENCE

Forces

KU-453-253

Robert Snedden

Heinemann LIBRARY

Schools Library and Information Service

S00000625499

First published in Great Britain by Heinemann Library,
Halley Court, Jordan Hill, Oxford OX2 8EJ
a division of Reed Educational and Professional
Publishing Ltd.
Heinemann is a registered trademark of
Reed Educational & Professional Publishing Ltd.

OXFORD MELBOURNE AUCKLAND
JOHANNESBURG BLANTYRE GABORONE
IBADAN PORTSMOUTH (NH) USA CHICAGO

Designed by Visual Image, Taunton
Illustrations by Paul Bale and Jane Watkins
Printed in Hong Kong

03 02 01 00
10 9 8 7 6 5 4 3 2 1

ISBN 0 431 03732 9
This title is also available in a hardback library edition
(ISBN 0 431 03725 6).

British Library Cataloguing in Publication Data

Snedden, Robert
  Forces – (Smart science)
  1.Force and energy – Juvenile literature
  I.Title
  531.1'13

Acknowledgements
The Publishers would like to thank the following for
permission to reproduce photographs:
Action-Plus, (Steve Bardens) p. 6; (Peter Tarry) p. 12;
(Glyn Kirk) p. 17;
Empics, (Matthew Ashton) p. 7; (Michael Steele) p. 10;
(Tony Marshall) p. 24;
FLPA, (E & D Hosking) p. 29;
J. Allan Cash, pp. 5, 8, 13;
Military Picture Library, p. 27; (Peter Russell) p. 18;
Robert Harding Picture Library, p. 15; (Explorer/JP
Lescourret) p. 4; (Brian Hawkes) p. 9; (Photri/Tom
Sanders) p. 11;
Sally & Richard Greenhill, p.28;
Science Photo Library, (Prof. Harold Edgerton) p. 16;
(Takeshi Takahara) p. 19; (NASA) pp. 20, 21; (Adam
Hart-Davis) p.25; (Simon Fraser) p. 26;
Trevor J. Hill, p. 14.

Cover photograph reproduced with permission of
Allsport (Vincent Laforet)

Our thanks to Jim Drake for his comments in the
preparation of this book.

Every effort has been made to contact copyright
holders of any material reproduced in this book. Any
omissions will be rectified in subsequent printings if
notice is given to the Publisher.

CONTENTS

Any words appearing in the text in bold, **like this**, are explained in the glossary.

FORCES IN ACTION

Forces push and forces pull. Forces make things move and forces stop things moving. Forces can make moving objects speed up, slow down and change direction. Forces press things together and forces pull things apart. Forces are at work whenever and wherever **energy** is being used.

Children in a playground exert a number of pushing and pulling forces.

Feel the force

Whenever you do something you are exerting a force. When you stand up you push back on your chair to move yourself up. With every step you take you push against the ground. When you breathe deeply the muscles in your chest force your chest to expand. When you turn the pages of this book you exert a force that pulls the pages up and over. And all the time there are forces acting on you.

Universal forces

Forces can act on scales that are both unimaginably big and invisibly small. Powerful forces hold together **atoms**, the tiny particles that make up all of the materials around us. The force of **gravity** keeps the Earth travelling around the Sun.

The force of gravity may be one of the weakest forces but it acts across the entire Universe.

Closer to home, gravity pulls you back down to the ground when you jump up. A force is something that acts on an object – and all objects, no matter how big or how small, have forces acting on them. Forces are acting on us all of the time.

Action at a distance

Some forces are only felt when one object touches another. When you kick a ball you impart a force that changes its speed and direction. If you missed the ball it would not move. It is a contact force. Other forces such as gravity and **magnetism** are non-contact forces. They can make an object move without actually touching it.

It's a fact – Nuclear force

The strongest of all forces work over the shortest of distances. These are the nuclear forces that hold together the tiny atoms from which all materials are made.

Try this – Force of attraction

You need: woollen clothes, a balloon, a helper

What to do: Rub the balloon against some wool and then hold it above your helper's head. Watch as their hair is attracted to the balloon. This is caused by an **electrostatic** force, which you produced by rubbing the balloon against the wool. Like gravity and magnetism, electrostatic forces can act at a distance.

FORCES IN MOTION

Everywhere you look there are objects in motion. Aircraft fly overhead, people walk and run, trees sway in the wind. On a grander scale, the Earth travels round the Sun, taking you through the year.

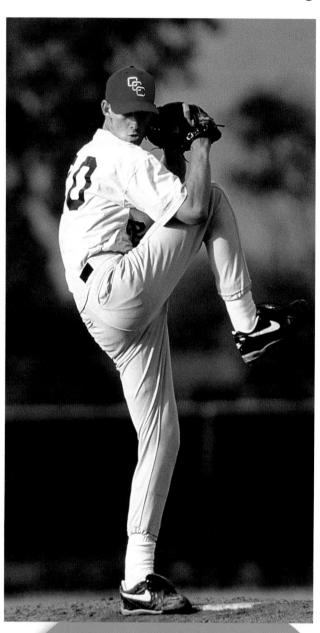

The baseball pitcher exerts a force that sets the ball in motion.

Newton's laws

Whatever form motion takes, whether it be the Earth's movement around the Sun, or the flight of a ball from your hand as you throw it, it can be described by three simple scientific **laws**. These laws of motion were discovered by Sir Isaac Newton.

Newton's first law says that an object will stay still or, if moving, continue to move at the same speed and in the same direction unless it is acted on by a force. The tendency all objects have to keep moving at the same speed and in the same direction is called **inertia**. Once an object is moving it will move forever unless other forces act on it. On Earth, the forces of **friction** and gravity stop this from happening.

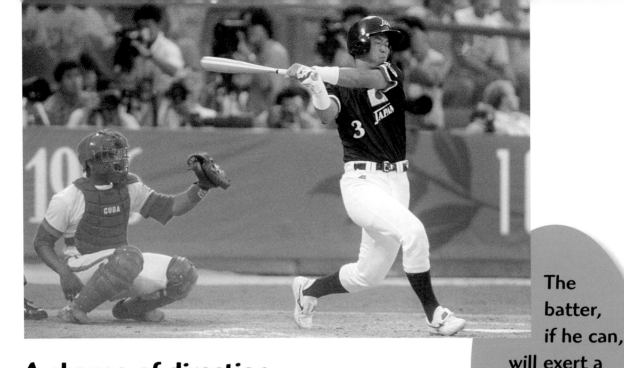

A change of direction

Newton's second law says that a force acting on an object will cause the object to move in the direction of the force. How far and how fast the object moves depends on the size of the object and the size of the force. If you hit a ball to the left you would not expect it to go right suddenly. Neither would you expect to be able to hit it very far if it were made of solid, heavy rock.

The batter, if he can, will exert a force that changes the ball's direction.

It's a fact – Sir Isaac Newton

Many people believe Isaac Newton (1643–1727) to be the greatest scientist who ever lived. As well as his work on motion and gravity, he investigated light and invented a new system of mathematics, called the calculus. The unit of force – the newton – was named after him.

Try this – Marbles in motion

You need: marbles of different sizes, a flat surface and a helper

What to do: Roll a marble along the surface and ask your friend to roll another towards it so that they collide. When they collide the marbles exert a force on each other. Watch carefully to see which directions they go off in. What happens when one marble is bigger than the other? Try side-on and head-on collisions to see what happens.

ACTION AND REACTION

Newton's third law says that for every action, there is an equal but opposite reaction. If you blow up a balloon and let it go, it shoots across the room. The action of the air blowing backwards out of the balloon produces the reaction that pushes the balloon forward. Whenever you push or pull an object it pushes or pulls you with equal force.

Jet propulsion

A jet engine also works according to Newton's third law. A powerful fan sucks air into the engine. The air is heated inside a combustion chamber, where fuel is burned. The heated air expands very rapidly and rushes from the back of the engine. This creates a reaction force or **thrust** on the engine that makes the aircraft fly forward.

Jet engines demonstrate action and reaction, producing a forward thrust by expelling hot gases backwards out of the engine exhausts.

Stopping a moving object

A moving object possesses **energy** of motion, called **kinetic energy**. Just how much energy it has depends on how heavy the object is and how fast it is travelling. In physics, **momentum** (M) is defined as the **mass** (m) of the object multiplied by its **velocity** (v), or M=mv. The momentum of an object only changes when it is acted upon by an outside force. A skilful fielder catching a fast-moving ball exerts sufficient force to stop it. The momentum of the ball is transferred to the catcher's hands, pushing them back as the ball is caught. The greater the momentum, the greater the force needed to stop the object.

A locomotive, which weighs several tonnes, has a great deal of momentum because of its huge mass, even when travelling very slowly.

It's a fact – Magnetic reaction

Newton's third law also applies to **magnetism**. If a piece of iron is attracted to a magnet, the magnet is also attracted to the iron with an equal and opposite force.

Try this – Balloon racers

You need: some balloons, lengths of cotton, drinking straws, drawing pins, sticky tape

What to do: Cut lengths of thread long enough to stretch from wall to wall across a room. Fasten one end of the thread to a wall using a drawing pin. Then pass the thread through a drinking straw and fasten the other end of the thread to the opposite wall. Blow up your racing balloon and then, keeping the neck pinched closed, tape the balloon to the straw. Let the balloons go and watch as action and reaction send them flying!

VELOCITY AND ACCELERATION

The speed at which an object is travelling is a measure of the distance it moves in a certain amount of time. If you cycle at a constant speed of 20 km/h, you will travel 10 kilometres in 30 minutes. Scientists tend to talk about **velocity** rather than speed. Velocity takes account not only of how fast an object is travelling, but also the direction it is travelling in.

Going faster

If a force continues to push or pull an object its speed will steadily increase. This steady increase in speed is called **acceleration**. A car picking up speed as it drives away from the traffic lights is accelerating as its engine pulls it along. A skydiver hurtling towards the ground is accelerating as the force of **gravity** pulls him or her faster and faster towards the ground.

The effort this cyclist is putting into increasing his speed is obvious.

The faster the speed increases, the greater is the acceleration. Acceleration measures how fast speed is gained – in other words, how many more metres per second faster you go with every second that passes.

These skydivers appear motionless relative to each other because they are all accelerating at the same speed towards the ground.

Terminal velocity

Earth's gravity accelerates a falling object, whether it is a skydiver or a dropped glass, at a rate of nearly 10 metres per second per second. This means that after 10 seconds the object would be travelling at 100 metres per second or 360 km/h. Of course, gravity is not the only force acting on a falling object. The faster an object goes through the air, the more the air resists it. Eventually the force of gravity and the air resistance balance each other out and the object stops accelerating. When this happens the object has reached its final speed, or **terminal velocity**. Terminal velocity depends on how much air resistance an object has – for a skydiver it is around 190 km/h.

It's a fact – Speed of light
The fastest thing in the Universe is light. It travels through space at around 300,000 km/sec.

Try this – Swing time
You need: a swing!
What to do: Sit on the swing and get swinging! As you move the swing forwards and backwards you are speeding up and slowing down all the time. You push yourself up and gravity pulls you back down. You accelerate as you push up, gravity slows you down, then accelerates you back towards the ground again and so on.

FORCES IN BALANCE

Why do some things stand still? That might seem to be a silly question at first, but all objects have forces acting on them all the time. If something stays still it is because the forces acting on it are in balance.

Balanced forces

Imagine a tug-of-war between two equally strong teams. Both teams pull as hard as they can but nothing happens. The forces they are exerting on the rope are in balance. They are pulling with equal force, but in opposite directions, and so the two forces cancel each other out. Even when you are sitting still on a chair there are forces in balance. The force of your weight presses down on the chair, but the chair does not collapse because it meets this downward force with an equal and opposite upwards force.

Sumo wrestlers are temporarily balanced as each tries to exert more force than the other.

Buildings and bridges

When architects and engineers design buildings and bridges they have to take careful account of the forces that will be acting on them. The forces have to be in balance or else the whole thing could collapse.

The complex structure of the Forth Railway Bridge is carefully designed to balance the load it carries.

A bridge has to be able to support the weight of the traffic that travels over it. A building has to be able to support the weight of its roof and everything it contains. The piers at each end of a simple bridge and the cables supporting a suspension bridge provide the upwards force, or upthrust, to balance the weight of traffic on the bridge.

It's a fact – How helicopters hover

A helicopter hovers because the uplift force of its rotors exactly balances the downward pull of **gravity**.

Try this – Building bridges

You need: two chairs of the same height, sheets of stiff card, some weights

What to do: Position the chairs about a metre or so apart. Place a piece of card on each chair so that half of it juts out into the gap between the chairs. Put a weight (a couple of heavy books, perhaps) on top of each card to hold it in place.

Put a third piece of card over the first two to complete the bridge. How much weight can you put in the middle of the bridge before it collapses? Try increasing the weights on the chairs. Does this make a difference? The downward force of the weights produces an equal and opposite upthrust that supports the two sides of the bridge. How strong is your bridge without the weights?

COMBINED FORCES

It is not unusual for an object to be acted upon by more than one force at the same time. These forces add together to produce an effect on the object. This combination of forces is called the **resultant** force.

Resultant forces

When you throw a ball, it follows a curved path through the air because there are two forces acting on it. First, there is the force you gave to it by throwing it. This sends it forwards through the air at a constant speed. Second, there is the force of **gravity** pulling it down towards the ground. The resultant force is a combination of the two.

Two people can combine the lifting forces they exert to move heavier objects than either could alone.

If the forces are equal and acting in opposite directions they will cancel each other out and the resultant force will be zero. The forces are balanced and the object does not move. Every time you pick something up you are producing an unbalanced force. You have to exert an upwards force that is stronger than the downwards force produced by the weight of the object you are lifting.

It's a fact – Strictly for birds

A bird flying through the air makes the air flow over its wings by moving them forward. This creates a lift that keeps the bird in the air, just like an aeroplane stays up.

Flying forces

When an aircraft flies through the air there are four different forces that need to be taken into consideration. First, there is the thrust provided by the engines sending the aircraft forwards. Second, there is an upward force, called **lift**, that pushes the wings upwards and keeps the aircraft flying. Third, there is air resistance, a frictional force called **drag** that slows the aircraft down as it pushes through the air. Finally, there is the force of gravity pulling the aircraft down towards the ground.

The thrust of an aircraft's engines propel it forward and create lift as the air moves across its wings. Streamlining reduces the drag caused by air resistance.

SQUASHING AND STRETCHING

Sometimes a force acts on an object that is not able to move. This may make the object change shape. The ability of an object or material to return to its original size and shape after being pushed or pulled by an outside force is called **elasticity**.

It's a fact – New balls, please?

When a tennis ball strikes a racket at speed it is squashed nearly flat by the impact. The ball's **momentum** is absorbed by the elasticity of the ball and the racket strings and is then returned rapidly as the ball springs back into shape, speeding away from the racket again.

Elastic materials

When you pull a rubber band it stretches as you exert a force on it. As soon as you let it go it springs back to its original shape. A rubber band is a good example of an elastic material. Some materials are more elastic than others – rubber is very elastic, concrete is not at all elastic.

Elastic energy

When you **compress** a spring or stretch it you are doing work. As you do so you are transferring **energy** into the spring. The energy you are storing there is called **elastic potential energy**. As soon as the spring can return to its original shape this energy will be released.

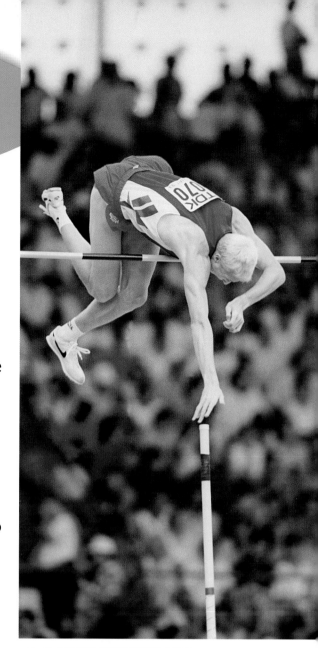

A pole vaulter is helped over the bar as the pole's elasticity springs it back into shape.

Elastic materials undergo **stresses** and **strains** when acted on by a force. The stress on an object is measured by the strength of the force acting on it. The strain is the amount by which the material changes shape. The higher the stress, the greater the strain.

Elastic limit

No matter how stretchy a material is, nothing can be stretched for ever. Eventually the material will either snap or just not return to its original shape. When this happens the material is said to have passed its **elastic limit**.

Try this – Elastic racers

You need: some model cars, some strong rubber bands, a long flat board, some thumbtacks

What to do: Anchor the rubber bands at one end of the board using the thumbtacks. Stretch the band back by pulling a car against it. As the band stretches it is storing the force you are exerting on it. Let the band go and energy is released as the band springs back to its original shape, propelling the car down the board. Experiment with different thicknesses of band and bigger stretches to see how far you can make your cars go.

FRICTION

Why is it difficult to pull a heavy object along the ground – but easier if it is on wheels? When two things rub together there is a force called **friction**. It slows things down and stops things moving. Friction occurs wherever moving objects come into contact. Putting wheels on something cuts down on the area of the object that is in contact with the ground and this reduces the friction.

A jet fighter uses a drogue chute to slow its speed through air resistance and reduce its landing distance.

Shapes and surfaces

The amount of friction there will be is determined by the shape and surface of the object. A ball or a wheel rolls freely because of its shape. Only a small part of the ball's surface is in contact with the ground at any one moment. An object of exactly the same weight and material, but shaped like a block has a lot more of its surface in contact with the ground. It will not move along the ground very easily because there is more friction.

All objects produce friction because nothing is perfectly smooth. Friction can be reduced by lubricating surfaces with oil or grease. Oil is added to car engine parts to reduce the amount of friction between moving parts. Otherwise the parts would soon wear out.

Air resistance

An object moving through the air collides with the tiny particles that make up the air and this causes friction. The faster the object is moving the more collisions there are and the greater the friction. This friction is called air resistance.

Friction is kept to a minimum in a car by using a design that reduces air resistance.

It's a fact – Getting hot

When you rub your hands together the heat you feel is caused by friction. When an object is slowed by the friction of rubbing it loses some of its **energy** of motion, or **kinetic energy**. Some of this energy is changed into heat energy.

Try this – Friction cars

You need: a model car, some coarse sandpaper, a table, some string, a small plastic pot and some weights

What to do: Tie one end of the string to the front of the car and attach the other end to the plastic pot, which should hang down over the side of the table. How much weight do you need to put in the pot to get the car moving? Put sandpaper under the car. Do you need to add more weight to the pot to move the car now? Does this mean that the sandpaper causes a greater friction force than the table?

GRAVITY

Another of Isaac Newton's great achievements was to realize that the force that kept the Moon in **orbit** around the Earth was the same force that made an apple fall to the ground – **gravity**.

Everyone is attractive!

Every object pulls every other object towards it through the force of gravity. Two cups sitting side by side on a table are attracting each other. But the tiny force they produce is overwhelmed by the massive force of attraction produced by the Earth that pulls them down onto the table. The size of the force of gravity depends on two things: the **mass** (the amount of matter it contains) of each object and the distance between them.

Flightpaths and orbits

The force of gravity pulls all objects equally. This means that two objects dropped at the same time from the same height will reach the ground at the same time. It does not matter whether one is heavier than the other, nor does it matter if one is travelling forward as well. A bullet fired from a gun on a level flightpath will hit the ground at the same time as one that is simply dropped. Of course, it will fall a lot further away!

Alan Shepard takes off on his historic flight to the edge of space.

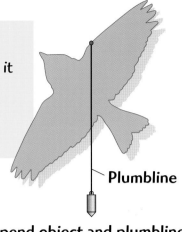

Plumbline

Suspend object and plumbline – draw line where plumbline falls

If a bullet, or any other object, travels fast enough, the curve its path takes will exactly follow the curve of the Earth. It is continuing to fall, but the surface of the Earth is falling away beneath it at the same rate. Instead of hitting the ground it continues on around the Earth. It has gone into orbit.

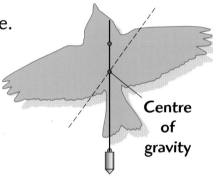

Centre of gravity

Suspend object from another point and draw line where plumbline falls again – centre of gravity is where the two lines cross

Centre of gravity
The **centre of gravity**, or centre of balance, of an object is the point where a single applied force could support it. It is the point where the mass of the object is equally balanced. Objects with a high centre of gravity, such as the average person, are unstable. If you lean too far back or to the side you will begin to fall as gravity pulls you off balance.

Finding the centre of gravity.

Try this – Balancing act
You need: a cork, a needle, two dining forks, a piece of string tied between two chair backs

What to do: Push the needle into the bottom of the cork then push a fork into opposite sides of the cork. Now try to balance the cork on the string on the point of the needle. It should be easier than you think. The heavy forks mean that the centre of gravity of your balancer is actually somewhere outside it, directly under the needle. This gives it stability.

Weights and measures

There are three ways in which you can change the weight of an object. You can take some of it away so it has less **mass** and therefore becomes lighter, or you can add mass to it so it becomes heavier. Or you could make it lighter by taking it out into space away from the Earth.

Weight and gravity

The weight of an object tells you how much the Earth's force of **gravity** is pulling on it. An object close to the Earth's surface weighs more than one that is far away from it. If you take your object to the Moon, which is smaller than the Earth and exerts less of a pull, it will weigh less. If you could take it to Jupiter, the biggest of the planets, Jupiter's powerful gravity would make it heavier.

Free-falling

A spacecraft in **orbit** is constantly falling towards the Earth without being slowed down by air resistance. As a result, the astronauts do not feel the

In the near weightlessness of space astronauts can move objects that would be impossibly heavy to shift on Earth.

acceleration of gravity but feel weightless instead. The orbiting astronauts and their spacecraft are not actually weightless. The Earth's gravity is still there but it is not felt as long as the spacecraft is in **freefall**. Space scientists tend to use the term **microgravity** to describe the forces inside a spacecraft as all the objects inside it are attracted to one another.

Newtons

Forces are generally measured in units called newtons. Ten newtons are roughly the force needed to move a mass of one kilogram on the Earth. One newton is about the force you would need to lift an apple a metre off the ground against the Earth's gravity. A typical jet engine exerts a force of about 100,000 newtons.

An astronaut would be three times lighter on Mars than on Earth because of Mars' weaker gravity.

It's a fact – Weight changes

If it were possible to stand on Jupiter you would weigh nearly three times what you do on Earth. On Mars you would have around a third of your Earth weight.

Try this – Instant weight loss!

You need: a set of bathroom scales

What to do: Stand on the scales. Hold your hands up at shoulder height then thrust them down quickly. Watch the indicator on the scales go down slightly. Your downward thrust is matched by an upward thrust (Newton's third law again) that works against gravity, making you momentarily lighter.

TURNING AND SPINNING

If you apply a force to an object that is fixed in one place, but which can turn freely, the object will rotate around the fixed point. This fixed point is called a pivot, or **fulcrum**.

A hammer thrower turns and spins, producing a centripetal force. When she releases the hammer the centripetal force is removed and the hammer flies off in a straight line.

Turning forces

The turning effect of a force depends on the **magnitude** of the force and the distance it is applied from the fulcrum. The further away from the fulcrum the force is applied, the greater the effect will be. Try closing a door by pushing near the hinges, the door's fulcrum. It is much easier to push near the edge of the door where the handle is.

Going round in circles

The propeller on an aeroplane, the wheels on your bicycle, a CD playing in a stereo system, are all spinning in circles. How is it possible to get continuous circular motion from straight line forces? Spinning objects are changing direction all the time. A turning force, like the one you applied to close the door, sets the wheel, or whatever, in motion. A second force, called the **centripetal force** pulls the wheel in towards its centre, pulling the wheel round and changing its direction continually so it turns in a circle.

Going for a spin

A **gyroscope** is a kind of spinning top that consists of a wheel and an axle mounted in a frame. When the wheel is set spinning rapidly it has **inertia**, just as any other moving object does. It will resist attempts to change its direction of movement. The axle of a spinning gyroscope always points in the same direction, no matter how the object on which it is standing is moved. Gyroscopes are used to help keep rockets and aircraft on a straight course.

Precession is a special force that makes a gyroscope tend to move at right angles to any force that pushes on it. If you press slowly and steadily on the axle of a spinning gyroscope, it will move to the right or the left, not in the direction in which you are pushing it.

A spinning gyroscope has a great deal of inertia and is difficult to unbalance.

It's a fact – Gyroscopes in space

Spacecraft rely on gyroscopes to keep them on course because magnetic compasses are no use in space where there is no Pole for them to point to.

Try this – Pedalling precession

You need: a bicycle

What to do: You can experience precession for yourself. Lean to one side while you are riding your bicycle, and it will turn that way even if you keep the handlebars pointing straight ahead.

FLOATING AND SINKING

Many things will float on water – from a huge oil tanker to a leaf on a pond. They float because they are being supported by the water.

Buoyancy

The upward push of a fluid on an object is called **buoyancy**. It is not just objects that float that are affected by buoyancy. As you lie in the bath try lifting a leg out of the water. Do you notice that it feels lighter in the water? This is because the water is supporting part of your leg's weight.

Oil is less dense than water and will float on it, a fact that leads to terrible pollution of coasts when tankers run aground.

Sink or float?

What determines whether an object will sink or float? It is not weight. A whole tree trunk will float just as well as a twig, but even a small pebble will sink. What determines whether or not an object will sink is **density**.

Density measures the amount of material in a given **volume**, calculated by the formula $D = m/V$, where D = density, m = **mass** and V = volume. Find a rock and a piece of wood of about the same weight.

The weight of the rock is concentrated into a much smaller space than the weight of the wood. The rock is denser than the wood. Fluids also have density. When an object is placed in a fluid, some of the fluid is pushed aside or displaced. If the fluid is denser than the object, it means that the object weighs less than the fluid it displaces, and the object will float. However, if the fluid is less dense than the object, the object weighs more than the fluid it displaces and it sinks. Drop the rock and the piece of wood into water. The rock sinks, but the wood floats.

It's a fact – Dive, dive, dive!

A submarine has special ballast tanks inside that are flooded with water when it wants to dive. This increases the submarine's density and so it sinks. When the submarine has to come to the surface again the water is pumped out of the tanks and it rises up through the water again.

Try this – Different densities

You need: a tall glass, a spoon, some syrup, some water and some cooking oil

What to do: Carefully pour syrup into the glass, pouring it over a spoon so that it does not get onto the sides. Next add some water and finally some oil, pouring slowly and carefully over a spoon in each case. The liquids separate into three layers because they each have different densities. You might want to try collecting a few small objects such as a cork, a plastic block, a piece of wood, and a piece of pottery and place them in the jar. Which objects float on which layers?

PRESSURE

What happens when you blow up a balloon? Why should you wear a cycle helmet? The answers to both questions are to do with **pressure**.

Distributing forces

What is pressure? To a scientist it is the force acting on a unit of area of a surface. This is not as difficult as it sounds! A force acting over a small area produces a greater pressure than the same force acting over a large area. If you wear a cycle helmet the force of a collision is spread out over a greater area, protecting you from serious injury.

Try pushing your finger into a noticeboard, then try pushing a drawing pin into the board. The pin goes in easily even though you have probably used more or less the same force. The point of the pin has a far smaller surface area than the tip of your finger. The pressure from the drawing pin is therefore much greater because the force you exert is concentrated into a small area.

Blowing up a balloon makes the air pressure inside it greater than the pressure outside it.

Air pressure

When you blow a balloon up the **molecules** of air in the balloon are moving around very rapidly and the inside of the balloon is being struck by these particles all the time. Every time a particle hits the inside of the balloon it pushes it out. Molecules in the air around hit the outside of the balloon all the time too, pushing it in. All of these tiny impacts added together are what produce air pressure. If the pressure pushing out is greater than the pressure pushing in, the balloon will expand.

A camel's big feet spread the weight of its body over a large area and stop it sinking into the sand.

It's a fact – Under pressure

The air in the **atmosphere** around us is so dense that the total air pressure on your body probably amounts to thousands of kilograms. The reason you are not aware of this huge force is because the fluid and air in your body pushes out with an equal pressure, balancing the air pressure.

Try this – Water pressure

Ask an adult to help you with this activity.

You need: a large plastic drinks bottle, a basin, a nail, water, sticky tape

What to do: Puncture a line of three or four holes from top to bottom in the bottle using the nail. Put a strip of tape over the holes to cover them while you fill the bottle with water. Stand the bottle in the basin while you fill it. Now quickly pull the tape off. From which hole does the water squirt furthest? It will go furthest from the lowest hole because of the pressure of water above it forcing it out.

GLOSSARY

acceleration rate at which velocity changes

atmosphere layer of gases that surrounds the Earth

atom one of the tiny particles of which all materials are made

buoyancy lifting effect of a fluid on an object that is placed in it

centre of gravity point in or near an object where the effect of gravity on the object is concentrated

centripetal force inward pulling force that acts on an object moving in a curved path

compress make more compact by pressing

density measure of the amount of mass contained within a unit of volume of a particular substance

drag force that slows down an object as it travels through a liquid or a gas

elasticity ability of a material to return to its previous shape after being stretched

elastic limit point at which any further stretching of an object results in it being unable to return to its original shape

elastic potential energy energy stored in a stretched object that is released when it returns to its original shape

electrostatic relating to objects that are electrically charged

energy capacity for doing work

freefall falling motion of an object that is being attracted by gravity, without being slowed down by air resistance

friction force that acts to slow down or stop objects that are moving against each other

fulcrum point or support around which something turns

gravity force of attraction between objects

gyroscope fast-spinning wheel, the axis of which stays pointing in the same direction once the wheel is set spinning

inertia tendency of an object to remain at rest or to keep moving in a straight line until it is acted upon by a force

kinetic energy   energy of a moving object

law   in science, a rule that tells you what will happen in a particular set of circumstances, for example the law of gravity, which tells you how an object behaves when acted upon by a gravitational force

lift   upward force that keeps a flying object, whether an aircraft or a bird, in the air

magnetism   force of attraction or repulsion that acts between some materials, such as iron

magnitude   measure of the size of a force

mass   amount of matter, or material, within an object

microgravity   small gravitational forces acting between objects that are outside the force of gravity of a large object, such as a planet

molecule   two or more atoms joined together

momentum   tendency of a moving object to keep on moving until it is stopped by a force acting on it

orbit   path an object follows as it travels around a larger object

precession   force that tends to make a spinning object move at right angles to a pushing force acting on it

pressure   amount of force pushing on a given area

resultant   force that results when two or more forces are acting on an object

strain   measure of the extent to which an object changes shape when a stress is applied to it

stress   force that acts on an object to change its shape

terminal velocity   velocity a falling object reaches when acceleration due to gravity and slowing down due to air resistance balance each other

thrust   propelling force generated by a rocket or an aircraft engine

velocity   measure of speed in a particular direction

volume   space that is taken up by an amount of matter

INDEX